presented to

Natalie (my best friend)

from

Beverly

date

9-17-06

a lifetime of *Girlfriends*

moments of innocence

by Bonnie Jensen

BARBOUR
PUBLISHING

Bonnie would like to acknowledge the generous contribution of
Anita Wiegand to this little book of friendship.
She is not only a joy to work with, but a joy to befriend as well.

© 2004 by Barbour Publishing, Inc.

ISBN 1-59310-576-2

Cover and interior images: Getty Images
Designed by Julie Doll.

Published by Barbour Publishing, Inc., P.O. Box 719, Uhrichsville, Ohio 44683, www.barbourbooks.com

Our mission is to publish and distribute inspirational products offering exceptional value and biblical encouragement to the masses.

Member of the
Evangelical Christian
Publishers Association

Printed in China.
5 4 3 2 1

In childhood, where we dwell in the world of innocence,
joy is as easy as a ride on the merry-go-round. . .
and friendship as simple as pushing each other on the swings.

How do you like to go up in a swing,

Up in the air so blue?

Oh, I do think it the pleasantest thing

Ever a child can do!

—from "The Swing"
by Robert Louis Stevenson

Stand on your tiptoes in front of the mirror,
and you are a ballerina. . . .
Put on a pretty dress and a plastic crown,
and you become a princess. . . .
Play dolls with your favorite friend,
and you are the happiest little girl on earth.

Say, Say my playmate
Come out and play with me
and bring your dollies 3
climb up my apple tree
slide down my rain barrel
into my cellar door
and we'll be jolly friends
forever more—more—more!

dollies

Conversation between childhood friends:

"I'll go if you go."

"I'll taste it if you will."

"You go first."

"Do you want the red gumball or the
    orange one?"

"Does your dolly have a cold, too?"

"Can you come out and play?"

play!

good things

He fills my life with good things!

PSALM 103:5 TLB

hugs

Friends treat us with love and kindness. . . .
They are God's way of giving us hugs.

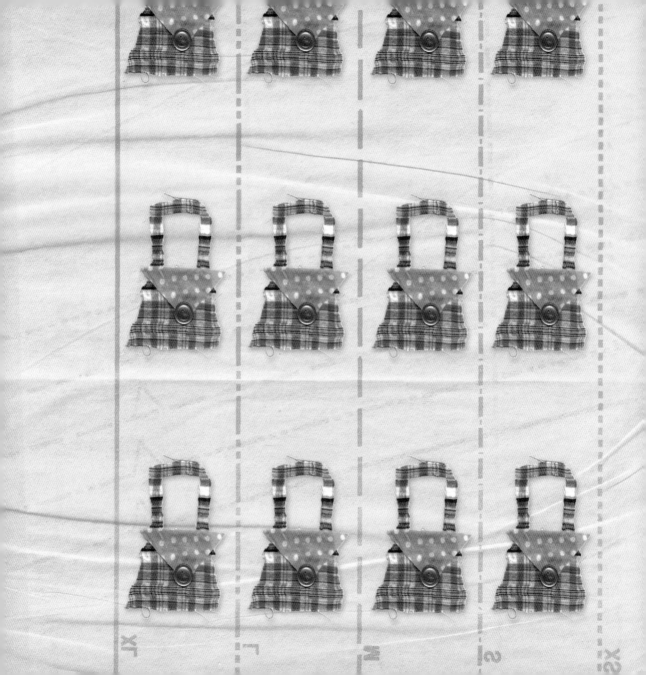

A child's wish:
I want to know about
the whole world and
everything in it. . .
and I want to discover
it with my friend.

How high is the sky?
How far is the east?
How can I number
   the sands piece by piece?
How bright is the sun?
How far to a star?
How long would it take,
   God, to get where You are?

Friends are like sisters
you choose for yourself.

When I grow up, I'm going to be
a nurse. . .or a teacher. . .
or a famous ballerina who dances
before the queen. . . .

A sweet friendship refreshes the soul.
PROVERBS 27:9 THE MESSAGE

Alice had begun to think that very few things
indeed were really impossible.

—*from* Alice in Wonderland
by Lewis Carroll

Friendship is. . .
picking your friend
to be on your kick-
ball team when she
would otherwise be
left for last.

friendship is. . .

The test of true friendship:
Packing your lunch when
you really wanted to buy so
you can sit by a special
friend at the "packer's table"
in the cafeteria.

true

remember

Remember when the world of
imagination was larger than life?

when. . .

Remember how exciting it was to
get a brand-new pair of roller skates
—and what a thrill it was to roll
down the sidewalk and show them
to a friend?

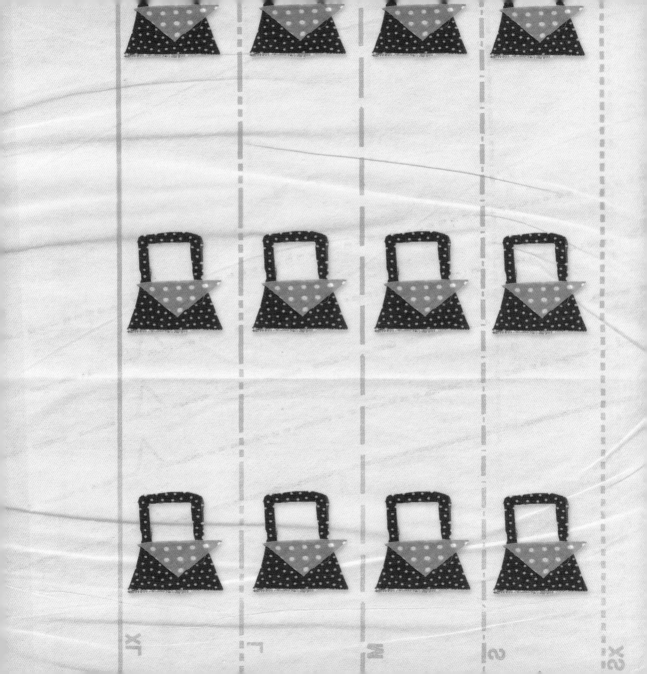

What does friendship
taste like?
A triple-decker ice
cream cone with all
the toppings.

Step back into childhood. . . .
Try to recall and recite a few of
your favorite jump-rope rhymes
(the friends you used to play
with will be in the memory, too).

Bubble gum, bubble gum,
in a dish. . .
how many wishes do you wish?
1. . .2. . .3. . .4. . .

Remember when your heart and mind were open wide
to new experiences. . .new ideas. . .and new friends? . . .
When happiness was a feeling you had every day,
and cares were as fleeting as dandelions in the wind?

It's a curious thing. . . .
When we are smallest on the outside,
we have the greatest capacity to grow
and learn on the inside.

What makes thunder?
How do airplanes fly?
Why don't spiders get caught in their webs?
Is there really a tooth fairy?

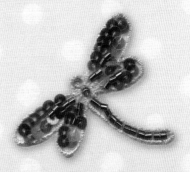

Red rover, red rover. . .
let my best friend come over.

best friends

Those were the days. . .chasing fireflies,
skipping rocks across the water,
picking flowers from the neighbor's garden. . .
Wait! I still do that!

adventure

always

There's always room in a child's heart for one more friend.

little girls

Oh, to be little girls again, filled with uninhibited emotion.

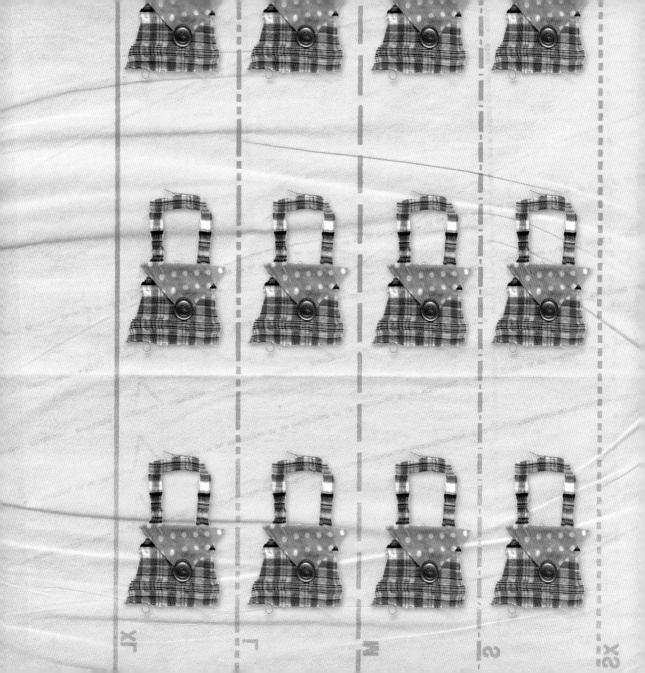

Revisiting childhood friendships
could make us better at being
grown-up friends—were we ever so
anxious and willing to help. . .
more excited to see each other. . .
least likely to stay angry, or quicker
to forgive?

Remember when bracelets made from dandelion stems were quite fashionable?

We didn't actually believe
that stepping on a crack in
the sidewalk would break
our mothers' backs, did we?

What is childhood made of ?
Pony rides and curly slides, and day trips to the zoo—
Happy days and carefree ways and friends who walk beside you.

Let's go back to "playing" house.
It was fun to do dishes, easy to
forget the dusting, and we usually
had a friend stopping by!

It will always be fun to
buy a new box of crayons,
catch a snowflake on your
tongue, and try on a pair
of high-heeled shoes.

There were days when she
ran in the garden, like a
child of ten after a butterfly.
—*Alexandre Dumas*

butterflies

The Lord watches over
the lives of the innocent.
Their reward will last forever.

PSALM 37:18 ICB

forever

rainbows

The world of innocence is a colorful one.
A child's perspective is like "optimism in a bottle". . . .
It makes the sky look bluer, the flowers seem
brighter, and a rainbow feel like God painted it just
for you.

dandelions

Could our hearts beat with any greater pride than
to see the dandelion bouquet we picked displayed
in a vase on the windowsill or the picture we so
carefully colored hanging on the refrigerator?

Remember the true meaning of giving. . .
giving a gift that was not bought
but instead found tucked away at the
back of a drawer or the bottom of a
closet where all treasures are kept.

We find delight in the beauty and
happiness of children that makes the
heart too big for the body.
—*from* The Conduct of Life
by Ralph Waldo Emerson

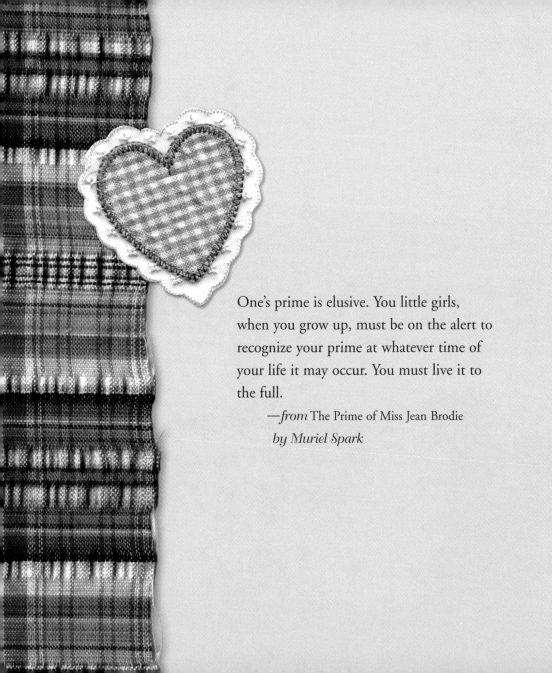

One's prime is elusive. You little girls,
when you grow up, must be on the alert to
recognize your prime at whatever time of
your life it may occur. You must live it to
the full.

—*from* The Prime of Miss Jean Brodie
by Muriel Spark

You know a part of you is still a child when you
give in to the temptation of walking through a
mud puddle instead of around it.

Our senses must be heightened
as a child. . . . I can't think of
another time when ice cream
tasted so good.

Hope
is
what
children's
hearts
are
made of.

So many things are exciting as a child.
Making new friends, discovering you like
the same things, learning they have dolls
you've never met. . . Life feels like one
adventure after another.

life is. . .

When a great
adventure is offered,
you don't refuse it.
—*Amelia Earhart*

an adventure

simple things

Teach us delight in simple things.
—*Rudyard Kipling*

always

A friend, once she's entered your heart,
will hold a place there always.

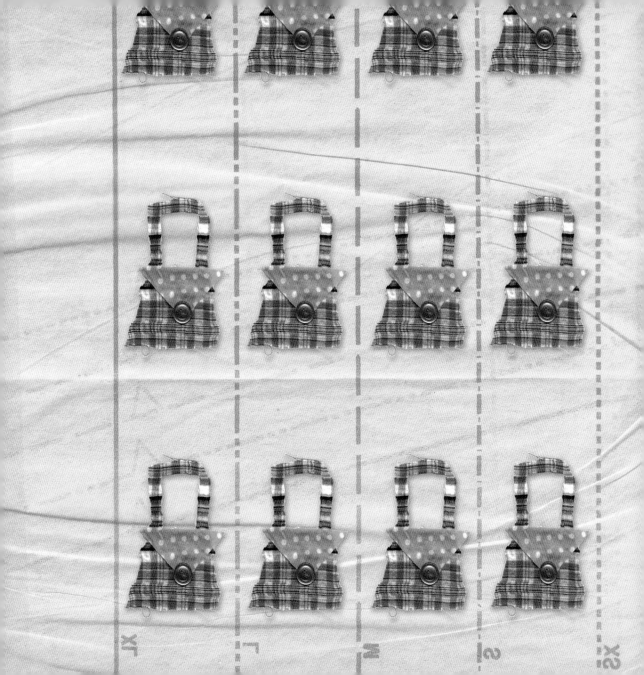

Wouldn't it be fun to
pick up the phone and
call a friend from grade
school with whom you've
fallen out of touch?

Eenie meenie miney moe,
Catch a tiger by the toe.
If he hollers let him go;
Eenie meenie miney moe.

A child's friendship is
the purest of forms.

Remember when recess was the best part of the day?
It was a "friendship" break—something we should make
time for even when we're all grown up!

Unto the pure all things are pure.

TITUS 1:15 KJV

Comfort was having
your best friend lose
a front tooth at the
same time as you—
there was something
soothing about looking
silly together.

As a child, a game of
hide-and-seek or a trip to
the park had the ability
to erase any sort of bad
day.

hide-and-seek

I have spread my
dreams under your
feet; tread softly
because you tread
on my dreams.
— *W. B. Yeats*

dreams

Laughter

Five Reasons Childhood Is So Much Fun

You get to laugh out loud without thinking
about how it sounds (or looks).

You get to see everything in the world with
amazement and curiosity.

You get to go through the day without looking
at a clock.

You get to ask a million questions and still
feel smart.

You get to believe that your life revolves around
your friends. . .and when you get to see
them again.

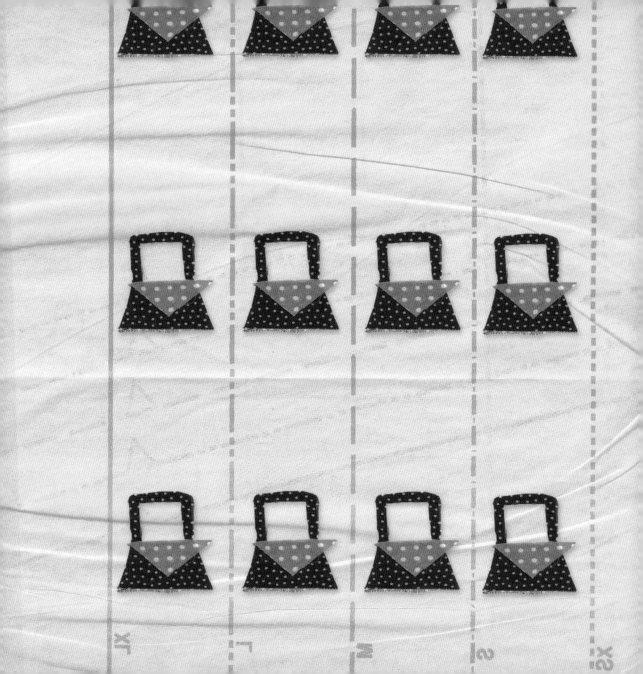

There are so many perks of being a child.
One of the best is the joy of spending a lot of
time with your friends. I remember being at my
best friend's house, marveling at her ability to
play the piano. I had always wanted to learn to
play, but my parents couldn't afford lessons.

Without hesitation, my friend sat down beside me on the piano bench, put her hands on mine, and began teaching me to play the simplest song she knew. I'll never forget that day or the song we played. It plays on in my memory of her and the lasting impression she left on me.

A friend is someone
who cares about your
dreams.

It is in childhood that we dare to dream the biggest
dreams while carrying the smallest reservations.

This is childhood. . .the season of being
free of cares and full of imagination.

Don't you see that children are God's best gift?

Psalm 127:3 The Message

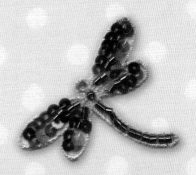

Jesus said, "Let the little children come to me, and do not hinder them, for the kingdom of heaven belongs to such as these."

MATTHEW 19:14 NIV

innocent hearts

Lord of hopefulness, Lord of all joy,
Whose trust, ever childlike, no cares could destroy.
Be there at our waking, and give us, we pray,
Your bliss in our hearts, Lord, at the break of day.
—*from "All Day Hymn"*
by J. Struther

childlike trust

grown-ups

Grown-ups never understand anything for
themselves, and it is tiresome for children to be
always and forever explaining things to them.
        —*from* The Little Prince
            by Antoine de Saint-Exupery

memories

Our friends are simply part of the cast as we
orchestrate a production of sweet memories
filled with happiness and laughter.

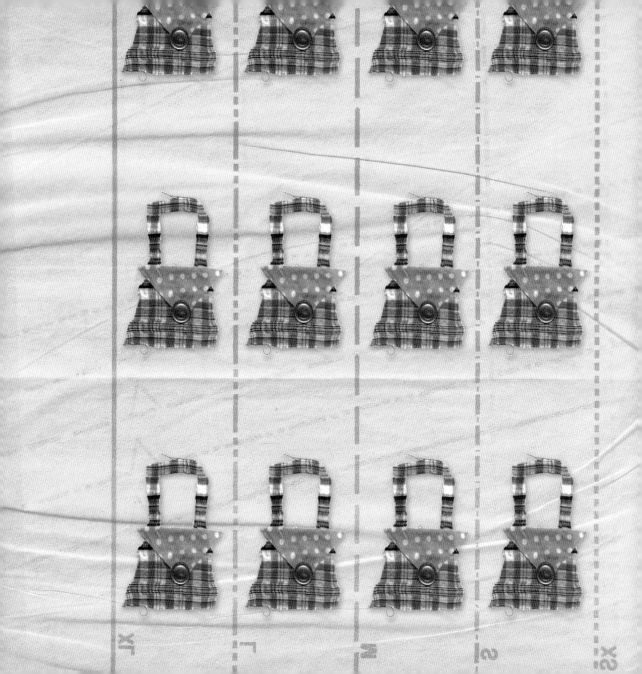

It was wonderful to be a child. . . . My friends and I had the luxury of believing that the world of pretend was as real as any other.

Remember when,
"How long can I
stay at my friend's
house?" was the
only concern we had
for time?

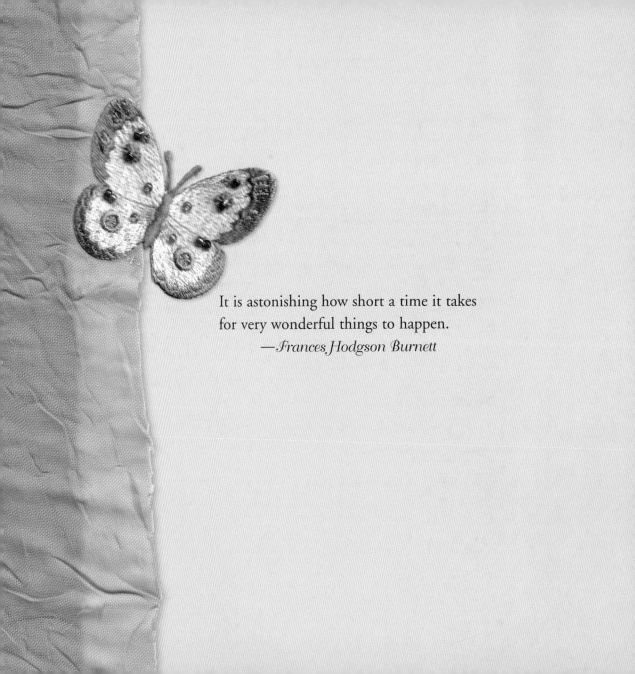

It is astonishing how short a time it takes
for very wonderful things to happen.
—*Frances Hodgson Burnett*

In friendship, it is never really necessary to grow up—
it is essential, however, to grow in our capacity to love.

Remember playing dress-up?
A floppy hat hiding the tip of your nose. . .
costume jewelry hanging to your knees. . .
lipstick the color of a ripe tomato. . .

To be a child is to greet each morning with anticipation and excitement. . .as if it's the first day of summer vacation or the day you bring home a new pet.

Remember when sharing your
heart meant sharing your
favorite stuffed animal with a
friend staying away from
home for the first time?

stuffed animals

Some of the best memories of childhood are those that can be. . .

felt—like the happiness my heart feels when I
   think of a special friend.
breathed—like the aroma of cookies just out
   of the oven.
touched—like the quilt made by my grandmother
   that hangs at the end of the bed.

smell of cookies

no worries

To have the mind of a child is to clear away all worries—and make sufficient room for ideas, curiosity, and dreams.

taking your time

Childhood is the place where trying to catch a butterfly is more important than being on time.

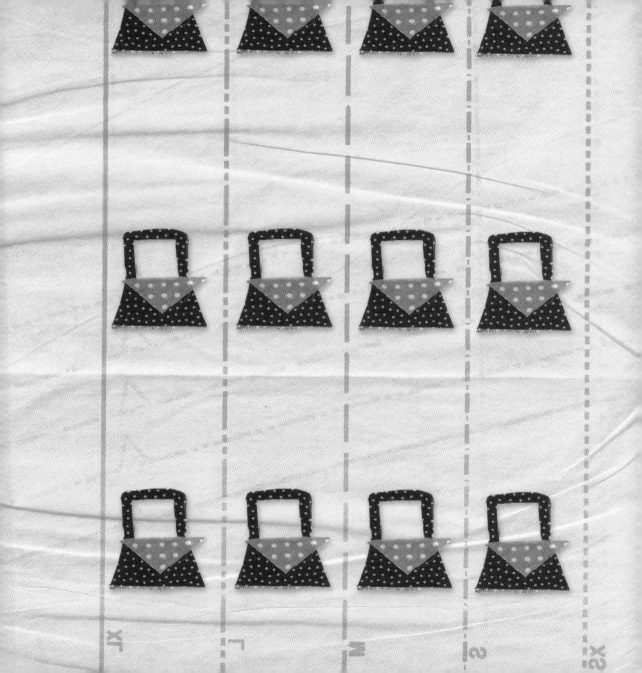

Teddy bear, teddy bear, turn around.
Teddy bear, teddy bear, touch the ground.
Teddy bear, teddy bear, tie your shoes.
Teddy bear, teddy bear, read the news.
Teddy bear, teddy bear, go upstairs.
Teddy bear, teddy bear, say your prayers.
Teddy bear, teddy bear, turn out the lights.
Teddy bear, teddy bear, say good night.
G-O-O-D-N-I-G-H-T.

In its innocence, childhood friendship knows no limits, no boundaries, no breaking point.

Popsicles. Cookies. Lollipops.
Some of life's most effective remedies.

A happy heart is like good medicine.
PROVERBS 17:22 ICB

Wardrobe musts:

> Shoes with clicky heels
>
> Jeans with fashionable appliqués
>
> Belts with gemstone inlays
>
> T-shirts with pink, pink, pink!

If you were a bird, and lived on high,
You'd lean on the wind when the wind came by,
You'd say to the wind when it took you away:
"That's where I wanted to go today!"
—*from "Spring Morning"*
by A. A. Milne

We must laugh
and we must sing,
We are blest by
everything.
—William Butler Yeats

sing

Free in spirit
and full of life,
A child's heart
is far from strife.

free spirit

snowflakes

A child's dream is like a snowflake before reaching the ground, before being influenced by its environment, before being reshaped beyond its control.

magic

There is something truly magical about friendship expressed through the heart of a child.

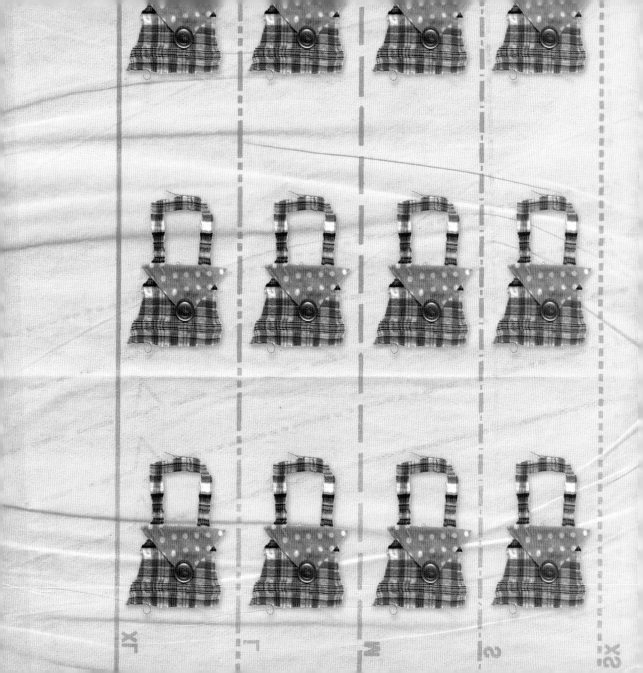

Let's take a bicycle moment. . . .
Remember riding without
    training wheels for the first time?
Remember being allowed to
    wander farther than the end of the driveway?
Remember wanting all the frills. . .
    a ringer, a license plate, a basket, colorful
    ribbons?

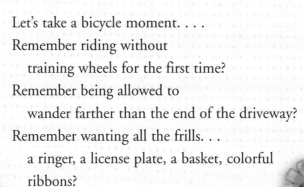

I would trade my
peanut butter and jelly
sandwich for tuna. . .
if it brought happiness
to a friend.

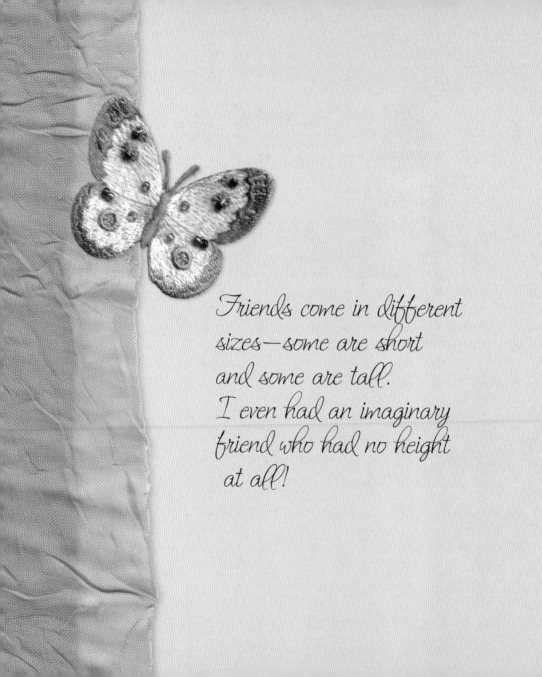

Friends come in different
sizes—some are short
and some are tall.
I even had an imaginary
friend who had no height
at all!

A tree house, a free house,
A secret you and me house. . . .
—*Shel Silverstein*

Childhood joys
go on without end. . . .